Fairy things to Stitch and Sew

Fiona Watt

Designed and illustrated by Katrina Fearn and Nelupa Hussain

Steps by Stella Baggott
Background fairies by Molly Sage
Photographs by Howard Allman

Contents

You can find out how to do most of the stitches in this book on pages 30-31.
Look on page 32 to find out how to sew on sequins, buttons and beads.

Flying fairies

Some of these plain materials are pieces of material that were painted.

Spread the glue thinly.

1. Spread white glue on a piece of thin paper, then lay a piece of patterned material on top. Glue pieces of plain material onto paper, too.

Draw the shapes on the paper side.

2. When the glue is dry, draw a dress on the large piece and cut it out. Draw a head, hands and feet on the other papers and cut them out, too.

3. Then, lay the head onto the paper for the hair and draw around it. Draw the hair around the outline of the head, then cut it out.

4. Sew a line of running stitches, along the bottom of the dress. Then, sew another line of running stitches a little way above it.

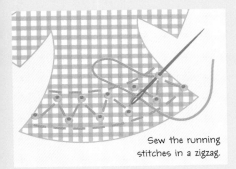

Sew the running stitches in a zigzag.

Find out on page 32 how to sew on a sequin and bead.

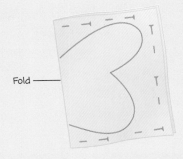

Fold —

5. Sew a line of diagonal running stitches between the stitched lines. Then, sew a little bead at each end of the stitches.

6. Then, push your needle up from the back on one side of the hair and sew on a sequin and a bead. Sew them on the other side, too.

7. For the wings, fold a piece of felt in half and pin it. Draw the shape of a wing against the fold. Cut around it, then remove the pins.

The running stitches on this fairy had beads added as they were being stitched.

8. Glue the hands and feet onto the dress. Then, glue the dress, face and hair onto the wings. Draw the face with pencils or felt-tip pens.

You could sew sequins onto the feet, too.

Fairyland garden

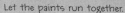
Let the paints run together.

Make the stalks different lengths.

1. Mix yellow paint with water, then brush it across the bottom of a piece of material. Then, brush pale blue paint above it. Let the material dry.

2. Cut lots of thin strips from shades of green material, for the flower stalks. Glue these along the bottom of the painted material.

3. Cut lots of circles for flowers from pink and blue materials. Then, cut out little triangles around the edges of some of them.

This picture had little cross stitches added around the flowers, too.

Find out on page 30 how to do cross stitch.

4. Glue the flowers onto the stalks and add another circle in the middle of some of them. Glue some flowers between the stalks, too.

5. Sew a cross stitch in the middle of a flower. Then, bring your needle up at the side of the 'X' and sew another stitch across the middle.

6. Then, bring your needle up at the top of the cross and sew a stitch down to the bottom. Decorate other flowers in the same way.

You could sew little beads on the flowers, too.

Hanging hearts

Keep the material folded.

1. Draw a heart on a piece of thin paper and cut it out. Then, fold a piece of material in half, pin the heart onto it and cut around it.

Use a pin to secure the small heart.

2. Cut out a smaller heart from another piece of material. Sew it in the middle of one of the big hearts with running stitch.

3. Tie a bow in a piece of thin ribbon. Sew it onto the hearts with several little stitches through the middle of the knot.

4. Pin the two big hearts together. Sew around the edges with running stitch, but leave a gap at the top, like this.

5. Twist one end of a pipe cleaner around and around to make a spiral. Then, twist the other end in the opposite direction, like this.

6. Push the pipe cleaner into the gap. Then, tear a cotton ball into pieces and push them inside the heart. Don't fill it too full.

Use the pipe cleaner to hang up your stitched heart.

7. Continue to sew around the edge of the heart with running stitch. Then, finish off by doing one or two tiny stitches (see page 31).

Fairy cake collage

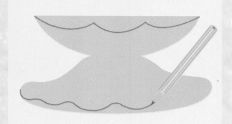

1. Draw a cake stand on a piece of material and cut it out. Draw three curves in the top and a wavy line along the bottom, and cut them out.

2. Cut a long sausage shape from a different material for the bottom layer of the cake. Then, cut curves into the bottom of it.

3. Glue the cake stand at the bottom of a piece of material. Then, glue on the bottom layer of the cake, leaving a gap between them.

4. Cut out lots of little 'D' shapes from another piece of material and glue them along the bottom layer of the cake, like this.

5. Cut out more layers for the cake, making them shorter and shorter. Glue them onto the material. Glue on some candles, too.

6. Sew a line of running stitches around the cake stand. Then, add some curved lines from the middle of the stand, too.

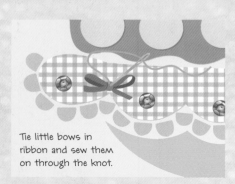

Tie little bows in ribbon and sew them on through the knot.

7. Decorate the cake with different stitches, sequins and beads. Look at the picture on the opposite page for some ideas.

8. Decorate the candles with diagonal stitches. Then, cut some cherries, strawberries and hearts and glue them around the cake.

9. Sew lots of little stitches for seeds on the strawberries. Then, add a cross stitch on each cherry. Sew beads and sequins around them, too.

9

This heart had little petals stitched on around the edge.

Heart and fairy collage

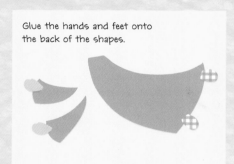
Glue the hands and feet onto the back of the shapes.

Glue the top sleeve onto the back of the dress.

1. Draw a curved dress on a piece of material. Draw shapes for sleeves, too. Then, cut out all the shapes that you have drawn.

2. Cut out hands and feet from different materials. Glue the hands onto the sleeves, and the feet onto the bottom of the dress.

3. Glue the sleeves onto the dress. Draw two wings and cut them out. Then, glue the tips of the wings onto the back of the dress.

This fairy's dress was decorated with cross stitches.

Draw the face with pencils or felt-tip pens.

4. Cut out a head and hair from pieces of material and glue them on. Draw the face. Then, cut out stripes for the dress and glue them on, too.

5. Draw a large heart and cut it out. Glue it onto a piece of material. Add two smaller hearts in the middle. Then, glue the fairy on, too.

6. Decorate the dress with zigzag stitches. Then, cut out shapes for the heart and sew them on with cross stitches and long stitches.

Pretty little bags

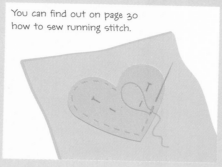

You can find out on page 30 how to sew running stitch.

1. Cut out a rectangle of felt. Cut a long strip the same length as the rectangle, too. Then, cut a square off one end of the strip.

2. Cut out a heart from a piece of material and pin it near one end of the rectangle. Sew around the edge with running stitch.

3. Tie a bow from a piece of thin ribbon. Stitch it onto the heart with several little stitches through the knot in the bow.

All these bags were made from felt, which doesn't fray when you sew it.

Match the edges of
the pieces of material.

4. Fold the long strip in half
and cut it along the fold.
Then, lay the rectangle along
the edge of one of the strips
like this, and pin it.

5. Join the edges with
blanket stitch (see page 31).
When you reach the end of
the strip, bend the rectangle
along the end and pin it.

6. Sew the edges together.
Then, lay the rectangle along
the strip again and pin the
pieces together. Sew along
the edge and finish off.

Start and finish stitching a
little way in from one end.

7. Then, lay the other strip
along the side of the
rectangle and pin it as you
did in step 4. Then, follow
steps 5 and 6 again.

Sew on any
sequins and beads
before you stitch
the bag together.

8. Cut two strips of felt the
same length for the handles.
Fold each strip in half and
pin them. Join the edges
with blanket stitch.

9. Open out the ends of the
handles so that they are flat.
Then, sew the ends onto
the bag with cross stitches,
finishing off inside the bag.

You could add
some toadstools.

In this picture, the sun
and grass were stitched
onto a background before
the flowers were added.

Stitch a spiral on
a snail's shell.

14

Fairy friends picture

1. Cut out three long stalks for flowers. Glue them onto a piece of material. Then, cut out some leaves, too and glue them onto the stalks.

2. Draw three flowers, then cut them out and glue them on. Sew a circle of material into the middle of each one with a cross stitch.

3. Cut a strip of material for a dragonfly's body. Then, trim the ends so that they are rounded. Glue it on beside one of the flowers.

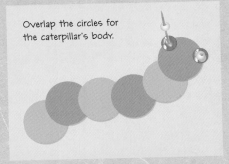

Overlap the circles for the caterpillar's body.

4. Cut out two large wings and two smaller wings from thin material. Dip the tip of each wing into glue and press them next to the body.

5. Sew two beads onto the top of the dragonfly's body, for eyes. Then, stitch beads along the body for patterns on its back.

6. For a caterpillar, cut out six circles from material. Glue them onto the background. Then, sew on sequins and beads, for eyes.

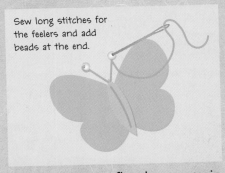

Sew long stitches for the feelers and add beads at the end.

7. For a bug, draw an oval body and cut it out. Cut out wings and glue them onto the body. Glue spots on the wings, too.

8. Sew long stitches on the body, between the wings. Then, glue the body onto the background. Sew on little beads for eyes.

9. For a butterfly, draw a pair of wings and cut them out. Cut out a body too and sew it onto the wings. Glue the wings onto the background.

Bend up each petal around your finger to make them curl, like the flowers shown here.

Flower cards

1. Cut a rectangle of thin cardboard. Then, fold it in half to make a card. Rip a square of tissue paper and glue it onto the front.

2. Open the card and lay it on a piece of folded kitchen paper. Carefully, push a needle through the card all around the edges to make little holes.

3. Glue a square of patterned material about the size of the card onto a piece of paper. Draw a flower on the material and then cut it out.

The stems on these pink
flowers are ribbons sewn on.
The paper leaves are glued on.

4. Draw another slightly
larger flower on a plain piece
of material and cut it out.
Then, thread a needle and
tie a knot in the thread.

5. Push the needle through
the middle of the large flower
then through the small one.
Then, push a sequin and a
bead onto the needle.

6. Sew back down through
the sequin and the flowers
and finish off on the back
of the flower. Glue the flower
in the middle of the card.

Tooth fairy purses

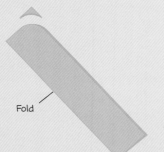

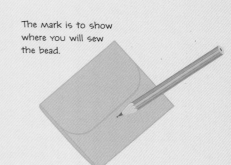

The mark is to show where you will sew the bead.

Fold

1. Cut a long rectangle of material and fold it in half with its long sides together. Then, carefully cut a curve at one end of the rectangle.

2. Sew along the straight end of the rectangle with blanket stitch (see page 31). Finish off with one or two little stitches.

3. Fold up the straight end of the rectangle. Then, fold the top down to make a flap. Make a mark below the middle of the flap.

You need a bead with a hole big enough for a ribbon to thread through.

4. Unfold the material and sew a bead with a large hole on top of the mark. Make the hole in the bead run from top to bottom.

You can find out how to sew these flower stitches on page 23.

These purses have lots of different ideas for patterns of stitches.

Make sure that the flap will touch the bead when it's folded over.

5. Turn the material over. Fold the straight end up again and pin the sides. Then, sew around the edge with blanket stitch.

6. Cut a piece of very thin ribbon and fold it in half. Use little stitches to sew the folded ribbon onto the edge of the flap.

7. Decorate the flap with patterns of stitches, beads and sequins. Then, push the ribbons through the hole in the bead to secure the flap.

Sparkly wand picture

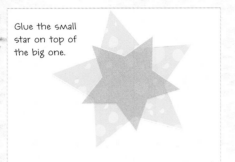

Glue the small star on top of the big one.

1. Draw a big star on a piece of material and cut it out. Then, draw a smaller one and cut it out, too. Glue them onto a large piece of material.

2. Cut a strip of material for the handle and glue it on. Then, draw very faint lines with a pencil, swirling out around the wand.

3. Then, stitch along the lines using a long stitch on the front and a short one on the back. Finish off with tiny stitches.

4. Sew on a long bead near one of the stars. Then, sew on another one a little way away. Add several more beads to make a line.

5. Sew more lines of beads coming out from the stars. Then, stitch little diagonal stitches along the length of the handle.

6. Sew double cross stitches around the wand (see steps 5 and 6 on page 5). Then, add some sequins, hearts and stars, too.

Dancing fairy collage

1. Draw a fairy's body in the middle of a piece of material. Then, fill her in with thick paints. When the paint is dry, draw her face with pens.

You need 15 petal shapes for her skirt.

2. Then, cut out lots of petal shapes from two different kinds of material for her skirt. Draw a bodice and cut it out, too.

Overlap the petal shapes.

3. Glue the bodice onto the body. Then, put a dot of glue on one end of a petal shape and press it on for the skirt. Glue another petal beside it.

4. Glue on five more petals, then glue the rest of them in a layer on top. Cut out four petal-shaped wings and glue them on above the arms.

5. Sew a big cross stitch at the top of the bodice. Then, sew more stitches below it until you reach the skirt. Stitch lines on her legs, too.

Push the needle down into the same 'hole'.

6. For a stitched flower, bring your needle up from the back of the material. Then, push the needle into the material again.

7. Push the tip of the needle up through material again, a little way away from the 'hole'. Then, loop the thread under the needle, like this.

8. Pull the thread gently to make a loop. Then, sew over the loop to secure it. Sew more stitches in the same way to make a flower.

23

Butterfly strings

Make the squares
the same size.

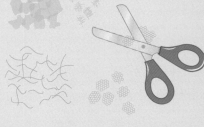

1. Cut out two squares of clear book covering film. Peel the backing paper off one of the squares, then lay it with the sticky side up.

2. Cut two or three long pieces of thread into lots of little pieces. Cut out lots of pieces of thin material, net and tissue paper, too.

Lay the film
sticky-side down.

Fold

3. Sprinkle the thread and material over the sticky film. Then, peel the backing paper off the other piece of film and gently lay it on top.

4. Fold a piece of paper in half. Draw a little butterfly wing against the fold and cut it out. Unfold the wings and lay them on the film.

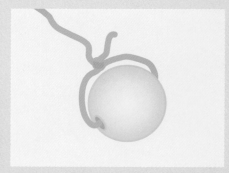

5. Press blobs of poster tack onto the wings. Press the wings onto the film and cut around them. Then, repeat this two more times.

6. Cut a long piece of thread. Push one end of the thread through a bead and tie several knots. Then, trim the short end off the thread.

Secure the
little bead a
little way above
the big bead.

7. Thread a needle onto the
thread. Push a little bead
onto the needle, then sew
through it again to secure it.
Add more beads above it.

Remember to
secure the bottom
bead each time.

8. Push the needle through
the middle of one pair of
wings and push it down
onto the beads. Then, thread
on more little beads.

9. Add more beads and the
other wings in the same
way, leaving short lengths of
thread showing in between
each set of beads.

Fairy pillows

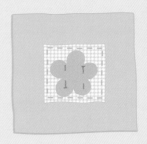

1. Cut two squares of material the same size. Then, cut a square of patterned material as a shape for the middle of the pillow.

2. Pin the patterned square in the middle of one of the plain squares. Sew around it with little running stitches, then remove the pins.

3. Draw the outline of a flower on another piece of material and cut it out. Pin it in the middle of the patterned square.

4. Push your needle up through the middle of the flower, then sew on a little button or bead (find out how to do this on page 32).

These silver beads were sewn on before the pillow was stitched together.

Make a rectangular pillow like this one in exactly the same way as a square one.

The heart pillow above had two hearts sewn in the middle instead of a square.

5. Pin the two large squares together and sew around the edges with blanket stitch. Don't stitch all the way along the last side.

6. Pull some cotton balls into small pieces. Push the pieces inside the pillow, but don't try to pack too much into it.

7. Pin the open edges of the pillow together again. Continue stitching with blanket stitch. Finish off and remove the pin.

Pretty rainbow

1. Draw a faint curved line across a piece of material for the top edge of the rainbow. Then, add more curved lines below it.

Let each stripe dry before you paint the one next to it.

2. Paint the stripes in the rainbow in shades of pink, red, orange, yellow, green, blue and purple. Then, let the paint dry.

Look at steps 5 and 6 on page 5 to find out how to do the stitches on this dark pink stripe.

3. Sew a line of running stitch along the edge of the pink stripe. Do the stitches close together so that they almost touch each other.

This yellow background was painted around the rainbow after the stripes had dried.

The clouds were decorated with little beads and then stitched on top of the rainbow.

The dark diagonal stitches on the purple stripe were sewn first. Then, the paler ones were added.

Use shades of threads that match the stripes.

4. Sew lines of running stitch along the edges of all the other stripes, too. Try to follow the edges as closely as you can.

5. Sew different patterns of stitches along each stripe. Use the ideas shown below, and make up patterns of stitches of your own.

Stitch ideas

Sew a line of cross stitch in a dark shade of thread, leaving spaces between the stitches. Then, sew paler cross stitches in the spaces.

Sew a line of running stitches. Then, bring a new thread up, next to the first stitch and weave the needle in and out of the stitches.

Sew two lines of running stitch next to each other. Then, weave the needle in and out through two stitches each time.

How to do the stitches

Tying a knot

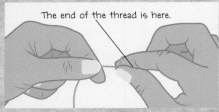

The end of the thread is here.

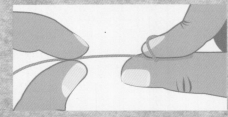

Pull the long end of the thread.

1. Hold the end of a piece of thread between your thumb and first finger. Then, wrap the thread once around your finger, like this.

2. Rub your finger hard along your thumb. You should feel the thread twisting and rolling between your thumb and finger.

3. Put your middle fingernail at the side of the rolled thread. Pull the end of the thread, keeping your nail on your thumb to make a knot.

Running stitch

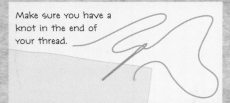

Make sure you have a knot in the end of your thread.

Keep on stitching in this way to make a line of running stitches.

1. Push the needle up from the back of the material and pull up the thread. Then, push the needle into the material a little way away.

2. Pull the needle down behind the material until the thread is tight. This makes a straight stitch on the front of the material.

3. Push the needle up from the back again, a little way away from the first stitch. Then, push it down again to make another stitch.

Cross stitch

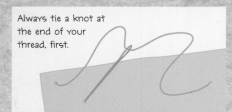

Always tie a knot at the end of your thread, first.

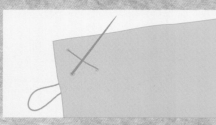

1. Push the needle up from the back of the material and pull the thread. Then, push the needle into the material at a diagonal, like this.

2. Pull the thread all the way through to make a diagonal stitch. Then, push the needle up from the back again beside first stitch.

3. Then, push the needle in beside the top of the first stitch to make an 'X'. Pull the needle behind the material until the thread is tight.

You can find out on page 29 how to sew these lines of wavy stitches.

This leaf has blanket stitch around the edge.

All the hearts have been sewn on with a cross stitch.

Blanket stitch

The knot is between the layers.

1. Lay two pieces of material with their edges together. Bring your needle up through the top layer of material, close to the edge.

2. Then, push the needle down through both layers of material, a little way away from the edge. Don't pull it all the way through yet.

Finishing off

3. Put the thread under the needle, then pull the needle down gently. Keep pulling on the needle until the thread is tight and makes a stitch.

4. Push the needle into the material beside the last stitch. Then, put the thread behind the needle and pull it again to make another stitch.

Finishing off secures the thread.

Push your needle through the last stitch and pull the thread tight. Then, stitch though the thread once more. Cut off the thread.

Buttons and sequins

Sewing on a button

1. Push your needle up from the back of the material, but don't pull it all the way through. Slide one hole in a button onto the needle.

2. Pull the thread up through the hole. Then, push the needle down through the other hole. Finish off on the back of the material.

If the button has four holes, sew up through one hole, then down through the hole diagonally opposite. Do the same with the other holes.

Sewing on a Sequin

1. Push your needle up from the back of the material, but don't pull it all the way through. Slide a sequin, then a bead onto the needle.

2. Pull the thread up through the sequin and bead. Then, push the needle back down through the hole in the sequin. Finish off.

Photographic manipulation by John Russell and Nick Wakeford